by Bethany & Scott Todd
illustrated by Kathrine Gutkovskiy

(c) 2020 by Scott and Bethany Todd
All rights reserved. Published by Lamplight Books, LLC.

No part of this publication may be reproduced, stored in a retrieval system, or transmitted in any form or by any means, electronic, mechanical, photocopying or otherwise, without written permission of the publisher. Such requests may be sent to contact@lamplightbooks.org.

First edition, April 2020

ISBN: 978-1-7346993-0-2

*For all the kids who face adversity and prevail.
Thank you for showing the rest of
us the way of hope.*

MATU IS BORN

Matumaini was born underwater at sunrise in Africa. She was just a baby hippo, yet somehow she knew not to breathe under the water. She held her breath as her mother nudged her onto the muddy riverbank.

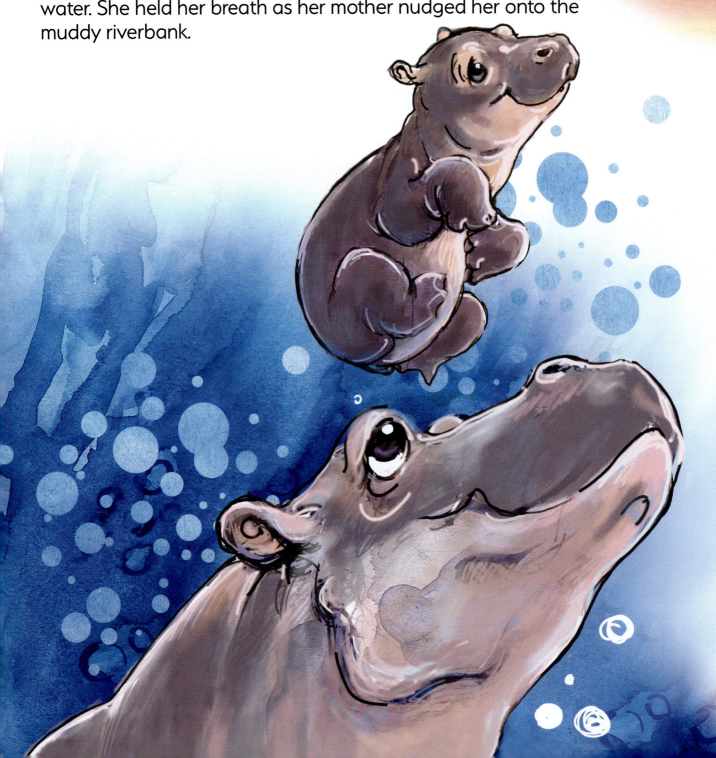

"Your name is Matumaini," her mother whispered fondly, "because you will bring us hope." Her friends in the hippo school called her Matu.

MATU LIKES TO PLAY

Little Matu liked to eat grass with the other baby hippos in her school. She enjoyed swimming and playing with her friends, and she snorted when she laughed. She loved feeling the squishy, brown mud between her stumpy, webbed toes.

Kanoni is Matu's Friend

Matu had a friend named Kanoni. Kanoni was a talkative grey bird with a bright red beak and crazy yellow eyes. He liked to stand on Matu's back and chatter away—talk, talk, talk! Matu usually listened to Kanoni, even though the bird didn't always make sense.

Kanoni Eats a Parasite

One day, a squirmy leech was biting Matu's forehead. Kanoni pulled it off and chomped it with his beak. It didn't hurt, but Matu still cried, "Yow!" Afterward, Matu said, "Thank you, Kanoni!"

"Parasites are yummy!" Kanoni replied. "But one time I ate a tick and it made me sick and that day I felt so bad that I didn't even want to fly but it was also a cloudy day so I didn't really want to fly anyway but..." Kanoni kept talking, but Matu stopped paying attention.

Hot Days

During the dry season, the grasslands became very hot. To protect themselves from the baking sun, the school of hippos stayed in the cool water all day. They waited until sunset to leave the river and graze on the grass. Without water, the savanna grass was turning brown. It was so dry and dusty that it made Matu's tongue stick to the roof of her mouth! She didn't like her food, but she ate it anyway.

Drought

The dry season seemed to last forever and the savanna grew hotter and the river became shallow. Some of the little hippos started to complain. "My back is burning!" one whined. His name was Kulalamika and he was always complaining.

Matu's back was hot too. She looked down and realized that she was standing in the middle of the river, but the water didn't even reach her plump tummy. It felt like the sun was sitting right on her back!

"Why is the river so small?" Kulalamika moaned.

"Drought," grumbled one of the adults.

Matu didn't know what a drought was, but it sounded scary.

THE MZEE

The oldest hippo was the leader. He was very brown and wrinkly, like a prune, and had wise but sad old eyes. Everyone called him "Mzee" and treated him with great respect because he was their elder.

"It is time to go," said the Mzee. "We must find deeper water downriver."

"What will happen to us?" The little hippos asked him. The Mzee didn't answer.

As the river evaporated, there was less room for the everyone. Scaly alligators were coming close to Matu and she heard one growl, "We're doomed!"

Matu's friend Kanoni said, "I have to find something to eat!" and he flew away.

The Migration

The river was so shallow that some places were only muddy puddles. Matu's feet were sore and very tired from walking so far. Kulalamika complained, "When are we going to get there? What if we don't find more water?"

But Matu knew complaining wouldn't help them find water, they just needed to keep walking, so she said, "We will find new water."

"How do *you* know?" Kulalamika demanded. "You don't know anything!"

Matu tried not to listen to him. She looked up at the sky and whispered to herself, "We will find new water."

Hunger

After walking for days, the river was gone and the riverbed was hard. Everyone was feeling grumpy, and Kulalamika kept complaining. "When are we going to eat?" he cried.

The Mzee replied, "When there is no rain, there is no grass to eat."

Matu said, "We will find grass."

Kulalamika gave Matu a mean look and called her a mean name.

The entire pod of hippos was discouraged as they stumbled over the dry, cracked ground.

"I can't walk another step!" Kulalamika moaned. "We're going to die!"

Kanoni's News

After sunset that night, a familiar grey bird with crazy yellow eyes swooped in and landed on Matu's back. "Kanoni!" Matu exclaimed cheerfully, even though she was tired and hungry.

"Hello, Matu!" Kanoni chirped.

"Where have you been?" Matu asked quietly, trying not to wake the other hippos.

"Eating dinner! There are tasty bugs at the lake."

Matu raised her head in surprise. "The lake?!"

"Chirp, chirp!" replied Kanoni, "It's just across the desert."

"Kanoni, we have been looking for water! Which way do we go to get to the lake?"

Kanoni waved his wing in a wide arch over the desert towards the rising moon. Then, he got distracted by a big, juicy fly and zipped off to chase it.

Matu stared at the vast, moonlit desert where Kanoni had pointed. The moon glowed dark orange on the horizon.

The Courage to Speak

Matu was very excited by Kanoni's news about the lake. She was eager to tell the other hippos, especially the Mzee, but she was afraid to wake them up. She decided that this was too important to let them keep sleeping. They needed to know!

When she woke up the adults they were very grumpy. Her young voice irritated the tired old hippos as she spoke, "I know there is water nearby. My friend, Kanoni, has been to a lake!"

"What? A lake? Where?" they barked.

Matu was nervous but brave as she told them, "We have to leave the riverbed and cross the desert."

The big hippos were startled. "Leave the river bed! We will be dead in a day!" one huffed loudly.

"What do *you* know, you're only a calf!" another criticized.

"You should know better than to listen to that crazy bird!"

THE MZEE FOLLOWS THE WAY OF MATU

The adults were unkind because they were tired and scared. But the Mzee was quietly considering Matu's words. He knew it was time for courageous action.

"We will follow the way of Matu," he announced.

The other hippos looked fearfully at each other, but they couldn't argue with the Mzee.

"To cross the desert, we will need to walk at night. It is too hot in the day," said the Mzee. "Wake the calves. Which way do we go, Matu?" the Mzee asked.

Oh, Kanoni better be right! Matu thought to herself.

The Night Journey

Matu turned to face the darkness of the desert. The Mzee stood beside her and said, "Do not be afraid. We will go into the unknown together."

Matu swallowed hard and started walking into the darkness. The Mzee was next to her, and the school was following them.

Matu could hear the chuffing of lions. She saw their shadowed bodies moving, and felt their gleaming yellow eyes watching her in the night. She heard the yipping of savage hyenas hiding in the darkness. Her heart began to race. There were strange and scary noises everywhere.

There was no path to follow. Matu didn't know how far they would have to walk. She felt the predators surrounding her in the dark, and she was scared of getting lost. She started to worry that they might not find the lake. Matu wanted to cry, but she didn't.

Doubts in the Night

During the night, questions and doubts filled Matu's mind. What if there is no lake? What if Kanoni is wrong? What if he pointed in the wrong direction? What if he can fly a lot farther than hippos can walk? What if the adults were right and we will be "dead in a day?" It will all be my fault!

Despite all her fears and doubts, Matu kept walking. Something in her heart told her to keep going.

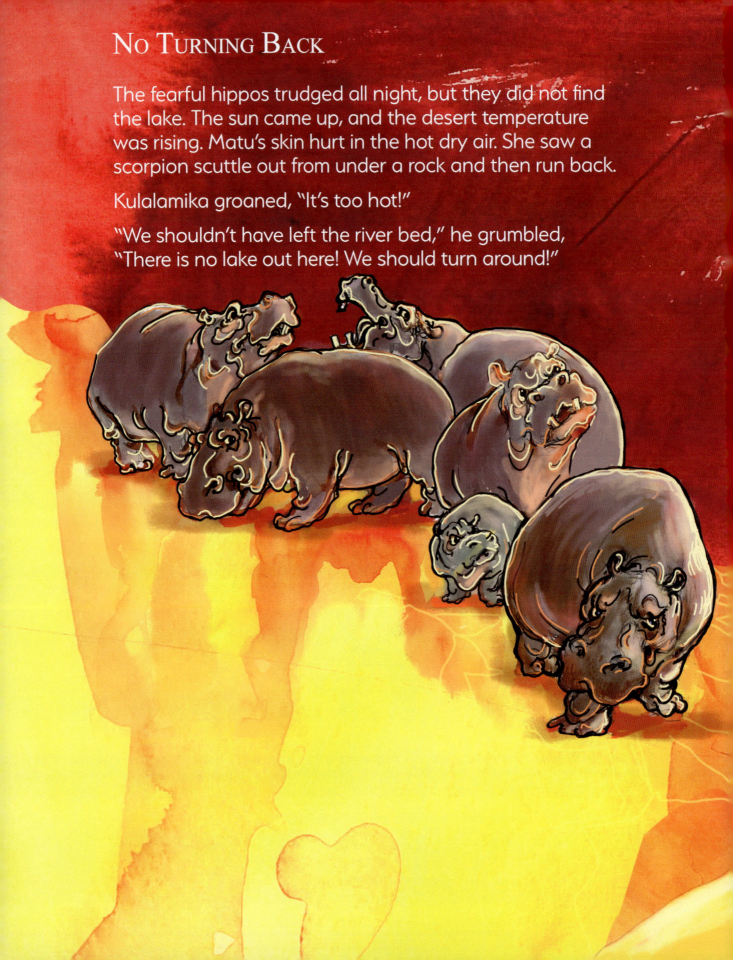

No Turning Back

The fearful hippos trudged all night, but they did not find the lake. The sun came up, and the desert temperature was rising. Matu's skin hurt in the hot dry air. She saw a scorpion scuttle out from under a rock and then run back.

Kulalamika groaned, "It's too hot!"

"We shouldn't have left the river bed," he grumbled, "There is no lake out here! We should turn around!"

All the hippos started arguing so loudly that no one could understand anyone else!

The Mzee turned to face the pod and declared, "There is no turning back now. Complaining does not help." But even the Mzee was having doubts. He thought it unwise to trust a talkative bird, but something about Matu made the Mzee believe they should keep going.

A Whisper of Encouragement

As the scorching sun rose to midday, the skin on Matu's back began to crack. A red juice, like blood, seeped out of her skin. The school was trudging slowly up a ridge, and Matu's heart was sinking with uncertainty. Then, she heard a beautiful little voice piping in her ear.

"Matu! Matu! Kanoni was right! Don't give up!" Matu looked around but she didn't see who said it. The little bird's words encouraged Matu just enough to get her to the top of the ridge.

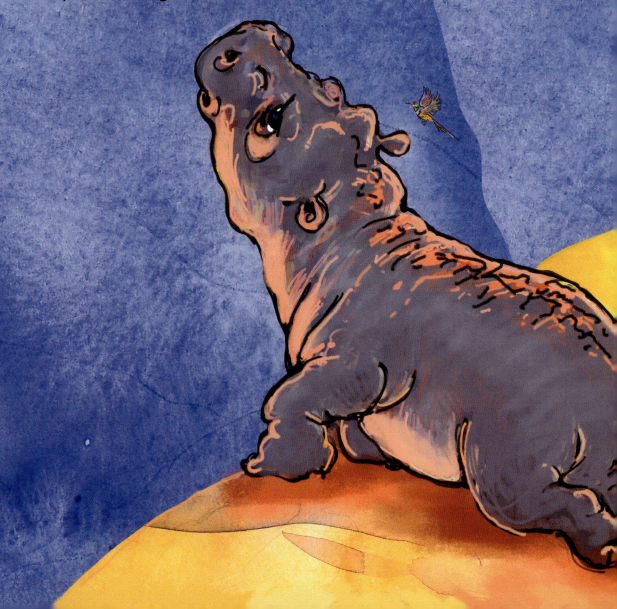

The Lake

Just as the hippos were about to give up hope, they finally reached the top of the ridge. Their eyes were wide with wonder as they gazed down into the valley. In front of them, surrounded by green grass, was a sparkling sheet of water! The surface of the water looked like thousands of shiny, golden butterflies all flapping their wings.

"Water!" Matu shouted joyfully.

Above the lake, they saw rain clouds forming, which made them even more excited. Was the dry season coming to an end? Were they dreaming? A new energy filled their aching muscles as the hippos eagerly rumbled down the hillside into the valley. Although they weren't to the lake yet, seeing the water made the rest of the journey a lot easier.

Water

The school of hippos reached the lake and plunged into the refreshing water. Matu smiled as her feet sank into the mud. She felt it squish between her toes. The beauty of the lake filled Matu with joy. Grasses were green! There were even flowers!

The hippos snorted and splashed and drank. They pulled up slimy strands of reeds and gulped them down. A flock of flamingoes launched from the far edge of the lake like a burst of pink confetti.

All of the hippos were happy, except for one. Kulalamika still had a grumpy look on his face.

Kulalamika's Regret

Kulalamika stood in the lake water, but his face was sullen. No one was talking to him. Matu walked over. "What's wrong?" she asked.

Kulalamika didn't want to answer. Tears came to his eyes.

"I was wrong," he confessed. "I tried to get everyone to turn back. And I'm sorry that I was mean to you."

"I forgive you, Kulalamika. What matters is that we're here now and the school is safe," Matu replied.

Just then, a wonderful shower of rain washed over the hippos. It was the end of the drought!

The Mzee and Mom Congratulate Matu

The Mzee and Matu's mother found Matu at the edge of the lake. "Well done, Matu," the Mzee said, with a twinkle in his wise, old eyes. "You did not give up, and that saved us all."

Then, Matu's mother said, "I knew you would bring us hope! I think I gave you the right name."

Matu smiled. And so did Kanoni.

About the Hopepotamus

All of us, especially children, need to believe that a better future is possible. And we need to find ways to get to that better future. But those ways are often difficult or scary. That's why hope is so important. Hope is not just wishful thinking or positivity, it is a belief that a better future is possible and the way-finding resilience to act on that belief even when (especially when) the way is scary.

The Hopepotamus was inspired by children who live in extreme poverty and yet find a way forward. For nearly two decades, the authors have worked for and with children who are malnourished, neglected, abused, coping with preventable illness or terrorized by gangs in the streets. The children who prevail in these harsh circumstances are the ones who persistently believe that a better future is possible and work to find a way to that future. That is the story of the Hopepotamus.

Matumaini is the Swahili word for hope. Something inside her says that there must be a solution, insists that there must be a way, and will not quit trying until she overcomes. She faces adversity, both the external challenge of drought and the internal challenge of doubt, with an indomitable spirit. The antagonist of the story is Kulalamika, whose name means "complaining", and he represents a voice that is undermining and threatening Matu's hope. Sometimes the hopeful person is disparaged as naïve, a dreamer or at least not "realistic" and yet people who believe a better future is possible are the only ones who ever get there – and lead the rest of us there.

The critical moment in the story comes when Matu chooses to set out in an unknown and risky direction. Similarly, children coping with adversity (and all of us) must face uncertainty and risk as we seek to overcome today's challenges and reach our envisioned good futures.

Dear reader, please encourage children to believe that a better future is possible. Encourage them to have a hope that is bigger than them-selves, a hope big enough for all of us. Tell them to never ever lose that hope.

OneChild is a global community of people working to help kids thrive. Join us at www.onechild.org and become a hope-builder for a child facing adversity.

Teachable Moments

Prompts for discussion with kids

1. Have you ever held your breath under water? How did it feel?
2. Do you think Matu was scared about the drought? Have you ever felt scared?
3. A drought is a difficult challenge, have you ever faced a difficult challenge?
4. How do you think Matu felt when Kulalamika was mean to her?
5. Why did Matu speak to the adults? Do you think that was hard for her to do?
6. What made the journey in the desert scary? Have you ever tried to do something you've never done before?
7. Why was the sunbird important in the story? Has anyone ever encouraged you to keep trying?
8. How do you think Matu felt when they finally saw the lake?
9. Why was it so important for Matu to keep walking and not give up?
10. Why did Matu forgive Kulalamika? What does it mean to forgive?

Fun Facts

- A group of hippos is called a "pod" or a "school".

- Did you find the sunbird on many of the pages? The sunbird looks a lot like a hummingbird but hummingbirds only exist in the Americas. Hummingbirds flap their wings up to 70 times per second!

- The names, Matumaini, Kanoni and Kulalamika are all Swahili words – do you know what they mean? (Hope, Talkative and Complaining). We recommend introducing these names to kids before reading the book.

- The Mzee (pronounced muh-zay) is the Swahili word for the elder or chief.

- Birds, like Kanoni (who is based on the oxpecker), help hippos by eating parasites.

- Hippos can run faster than humans, at 19 miles per hour.

- Hippos are actually dangerous animals and can be very aggressive.

- Hippos don't technically swim, they are too dense. They bounce off the bottom of the river or lake. Some hippos weigh up to 8000 pounds!

- Hippos can sleep underwater but in their sleep they have a reflex that makes them surface every five minutes to get a breath of air.

- In east Africa there are "rainy seasons" and "dry seasons" and drought is a serious problem.

- Climate change is a threat to animals and to humans, we all depend on rain.

- Rain signifies blessing in East Africa.

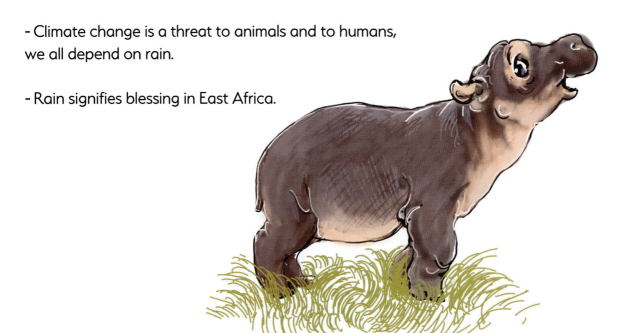

About the Authors

Bethany Todd has over 20 years of experience teaching children, kindergarten through fourth grade, in the United States. Dr. Scott C. Todd has over 15 years of experience leading holistic child development for children facing adversity and extreme poverty globally. He currently serves as President for OneChild, a child development organization serving 40,000 children in 14 countries. They raised their four sons in their home state of Colorado.